Memory Flood

For Lee who knew I would have a book long before I did.

Memory Flood

Poetry of Joe LaBreck

Goldfish Press

Seattle

Published by
Goldfish Press, Seattle

4545 42nd Avenue SW
Suite 211
Seattle, WA 98116

Manufactured in the United States of America

ISBN-13: 978-0971259898
ISBN-10: 0971259895

Library of Congress Catalog Card Number: 2017940919

Acknowledgements:

Many of these poems have appeared in the following journals:

Bellowing Ark, Stringtown, Riverrun, Chrysanthemum, The Oregonian, The Aurorean, Spindrift, Five Willows Literary Review, ByLine, and PKA's Advocate.

Cover photo credits: Joe LaBreck

Table of Contents

Fanfares

There is a late snow
And so there is no
Daffodil Festival.

The stems are frozen
And the blooms
Won't open.

Yet I hear
Muted yellow fanfares
Across the white.

In the Nature of a Shadow

It's January, and yesterday
There was a tree-destroyer wind.

Today is still and sunny
And I go into the woods to clean.

I build a pile of fallen limbs
Downhill beside the creek, and then

Within a pool of sunlight, use
My chain saw on a hemlock that blew down.

Suddenly I have a timid-wary feeling,
When a shadow moves upon my face.

Now I have felt the heavy
Darkness of a passing cloud, and flown

So quickly with a passing jet,
But this is very different, and I squint

Against the ridgetop sun and find
I look into a dark that is a deer.

5 Feb 98

First robin. I'm out burning winter limbs
when the chirping startles me. It's too soon.
There are no wildflowers, no new leaves.
I'm not ready to give the woods back.

In my snug home the television brings
talk about the effects of El Nino.
I have mowed leaves from the lawn, bought seeds,
tossed the baseball in the yard in the lengthening evening.

But I am millenia removed from what brought
a robin to this place at this time. I ask,
"What is wisdom?" and recognize in asking
I'm not wise about what the robin just knows.

steadyrain

eave   drip
leaf   drop

even   spreading
windless   patter

roof   rhythm
puddle   trampoline

washrag   sky
steady   wrung

gutter   purring
downspout   burble

curtain   falling
sleepy   blanket

steady   raining
steadyrain

Kaleidoscope

The sky changes the lake picture
Shifting from white below the rain
Showing tree browns and greens, as clouds
Open and pass the mountainside,
And when they break the sun reveals
Man's painted works in a green mirror.

The Crack of Spring

The cracking of the peat moss mulch
As sunshine sparks the soil to life
Gives hints of growth that starts below.

I walk this same way every day
And note the sunlit minutes spread
And feel the weather shift so slow.

If I would stop and finger dig
I'd see which green is pushing up,
But I'm content to wait to know.

Cascara

This spring we'll peel cascara, chittum bark.
I'll pass the lore of this one tree to a new generation.
It's a natural thing to do, and I'm the native.
Strip mall kids aren't taught this skill.

Our woods has lots of untouched bark
missed the last time bark thieves made a quick visit.
They only stripped the lower trunk bark, left
the trees to die. I'll show him the right way.

We'll get as close as we can by truck, then
pack in our bark spuds, ropes, lots of snacks, frozen
water bottles, and the chain saw. Know-how
includes the use of modern tools.

I'll say, "There's the first tree," show him gray bark
that is mottled, leaves rounder than alder.
He can show me the next tree, learn the forest
one tree at a time. There aren't that many kinds.

I'll test one limb to see that the bark slips.
Then we'll peel the trunk. The sharp nose
of the spud is used to make one slit through the bark
down the trunk from as high as you can reach

to near the ground. Then the dished end
of the knife is rocked back and forth down the cut
on both sides to start loosening the bark.
The rest of the work is done by the hands.

You have to push your fingers under the bark
around the trunk like you were going to strangle
the tree. Your hands slide in the cool sap.
Its wetness lets the bark slip off the trunk.

But you have to look for bumps on the bark.
They warn of protruding trunk spurs that lacerate
finger tips if you slide your hands too fast,
if your fingers don't read the tree trunk's braille.

It'll teach him control, balance of slow/fast,
sensing jaggers, stopping on contact, one
finger moving up or down while seven
slide on, efficiently peeling off the bark.

It is the sap that brings nutrients up the tree
building the epithelial layer growth ring, that yearly
circle of life. But when you peel the cascara
it is the sap that also allows its death.

After the trunk bark pops off in a long cylinder
he'll climb the spiral staircase branches high up the tree.
I'll get the chain saw, tell him it'll scare the bears
and cougars as it chews the wood, chews the silence.

Cascara branches form a wide ball top
that's a bouncy cushion when the tree falls.
He'll hold on tight when the tree rushes down, find some fun
in the hard work, build his trust and courage.

When I cut the tree I'll leave a six inch stump
with thick bark intact. New shoots will start there
and let the tree be reborn with several new trunks,
new trees for the next child to learn to peel.

When the tree is on the ground we'll peel the branches
down to a diameter of one inch. Then we'll pack
the cylinders of bark inside each other from smallest
to largest, making tight rolls to tie inside our rope to carry out.

The bark's inner side is shiny yellow
like the calyx of the spring skunk cabbage
that may be nearby. Orange salmonberries
are ready to pick, but you have to be careful

about putting your fingers in your mouth
when you eat the berries. Cascara is made into laxative.
There's a family story of a pet dog, left in a room
with dried cascara, that plastered the walls and floor.

Out in the woods talk can loosen, like the bark.
Knowledge of bracken fern and maple leaf
toilet paper may also be passed. Coarse amusements
liven the long day, postpone the tiredness.

We'll peel and roll and drink and snack
and cut and ride until we tire, or get as much bark
as we care to pack out to the truck.
And then our job is only partly done.

At home we'll need to spread the bark to dry
in sun on the carport roof, folding back rolls
to expose the yellow wet side for several days
with no rain, until the bark is dry enough to break.

Then it's cracked by hand into inch size chunks
that are stomped tightly into gunny sacks, used
to carry the cascara to the bark shed where it's sold.
Seventy cents a pound is what he'll earn.

Only then is there a payoff, money
in his hand for work he performed. Productive
labor, not chores, not allowance or a hand out.
There's still no law that says kids can't peel bark.

He'll pay no income tax on the cash he'll earn
bark peeling, or maybe picking wild blackberries,
cutting salal and ferns, gathering cones, gathering
dollars until they become hundreds.

This spring I'll take him out to peel the bark,
pass the skills on, show him how to use time for work,
turn work into money, invest it in chain saw
or drug stock, teach little money how to grow big.

Childhood Immunization

Before entering school
You have to present proof
Of immunization. Here is mine.

Drug withdrawals at birth,
Lack of hugs, hunger, cold,
Scary noises through the walls,

Being left alone,
Wandering the neighborhood,
Then lots of yelling.

A favorite blanket lost,
Pets that disappeared,
A blur of guys called dad,

Burns, stitches, a broken arm,
Thrown against a wall. That's
How I was immunized.

Now I'm ready for school.

Innocence Clock

Do you hear the alarm
of the clock of the young;
the striking hand and beat
of the belt; the knelling
spell of violent songs;
the clatter of tock in
four-letter words; the tick
of spoons in empty bowls;
the click of triggers and
firing pins; bong of denial
of drugs in the home;
the ad-page notch of the
underwear crotch; deadening
whir of a time bomb life
that deafens the young to
chiming time and timeless
life; the alarming sounds
of the innocence clock?

On the Swing Set at the Beach

The ponytail, re-colored blonde
Flies out behind her as she swings.
Her cut-short sweatshirt riding up
Displays her thong within the gap
Above pajama fashion-pants.

In edgy motion, swinging quick
She chatters with her protege,
A junior version tag along,
Until she drags her feet in sand
And halts to reach inside her bag.

The chains pull tight as she lights up,
Butt-braced against the seat, inhales
And holds a practiced pose, wrist cocked
Just so, two fingers high, turning
In her swaying, and yet unstained.

The Makings

She leaps
  in a feet out butt drop
    from floating dock
      to inner tube,

and sticks it,
  sitting pretty
    with a damp grin
      on the outrippling lake,

while her swimsuit crew
  pump their arms
    twist-leap
      and cheer,

in celebratory ripples
  of bonding warmth
    that are the makings
      of a joyful day.

Three Miles of Your Life

So you're looking across the Sound
At Dash Point while swimming
In that cool water on a really hot day
With a bunch of other teen-agers

And someone says it's not that far, which is
All the catalyst your adolescent chemistry
Needs. Before you know it you are the one
Who starts to swim across with your one

True friend, who would follow you anywhere.
Marco Polo traveled for years and got back home
To write of a great adventure. Columbus
Pointed west and just kept going. Our pioneers

Came across the plains. They saw distant
Blue mountains and a month later still
Weren't there. But there were no good
Alternatives to going on. So you swim on,

And your muscles count the strokes, and your
Blood gauges the water temperature, and your
Heart times the slow approach of the far shore,
And your mind begins to consider three miles

And how big a part of your whole life it can be.

It Should Always Be As It Is Right Now

We enter the Harborena, a gymlike gem
of tall ceiling and hardwood floor,
ancient glitter ball and black light
shining down on innocent white,
that has lit the skating, teen dances, and
roller hockey for multiple generations,
with pictures on the snack bar wall
reminding of occasions past when music
echoed off the concrete block walls
and filled the room just like Carl plays it today,
the Bird, Hokey Pokey and the birthday song.

This day it's two hours devoted to just you,
seven year old Jordan, and twenty friends.
The bell clangs as the lighted board changes
from Grand March to Couples to Reverse
to All Skate. As you loop the floor on your in-lines
do your eyes find the smiles all around
as grandparents, young parents and friends
gather on the benches behind the rails,
to catch up on each other's lives, or walk the floor
to help three-year-olds stand tall, and give comfort
to those who fall? Do you hear the joyous calls
of cousins, classmates and neighbors? Are the cake
and drinks at the snack bar table exactly right?
Do you find the opening of presents
in the middle of the floor even more fun
than the pin ball you played there earlier?

This year you open presents slower because
you can read every card. There are five dollar bills,
a labyrinth maze, Nerf rockets to throw, and of course
a game starts before opening finishes. And I watch
this moment of packages with hope that it can remain
a precious gift for you, a memory of how life
can be a present, even in a concrete block box,
when it's wrapped in the joy of children.

Living in a carbonated bubble

See that fat boy
down by the pool?
There's your symbol
of America today.
Fifteen, and four inches
of flab already hanging
over the top of his swimsuit
displaying
a shimmering, pierced belly button
bullseye,
inviting three in the ten ring,
a jiggly consumer
of government approved goods
with a big gulp worldview,
fat target for every hungry terrorist,
and ignorant of the wolf at the door.

Tourist Agates

They're inconsequential rocks
Tide-drawn smoothed on gritty sand and
Lying on the beach as pale shine.

They're scarce among the other stones
And hard to see in faded light,
But when they glint wet, angling sun

To your eyes, they have attractive
Brightness, and in a windowsill
Snifter they hold beach memories

Far better than a souvenir
Purchased in a curio store.

Learning to Write Nature Poetry

We sit in the poetry room and listen
About how to put nature on paper
While a deer nibbles into the clearing outside.
The poetry room has animal hides scattered on its walls.

We sit in the poetry room and talk.
Beyond our windows birds chirp and swoop
And feed babies in nests under the eaves.
The poetry room has a dry hawk suspended on a string.

We sit in the poetry room and read
While the wind sends white-topped waves across the lake
And scatters sun through a reflected hill of trees.
The poetry room has bleached skulls in glass cases.

We sit in the poetry room and discuss
While screams rise from a game below
Where feet pound the ground to beat a ball.
The poetry room has a sturdy table and comfortable chairs.

All Parts of the Circle

Each time I sit in the circle
I choose a different stop, a
random point on the gauge of time,
a lucky spot on fortune's wheel,

shopping for new points of view, new
shoulders that I'll rub. Does moving
put me in my place, or
will I find it if I stay?

Deep In My Woods

I see the quiet forest all around.
The silence from the leaves is like a kiss
that shuts the riot out without a sound
and focuses my view to my abyss,
a barricaded life against intense
compassion, walled through practice over time,
a gift I knew I needed, that presents
a sense of sanity, which has a rhyme
and reason, since it works. The deaths are found
in African machete arcs, a train
that roars across a boy, a family's last
vacation drive. And how do I explain
that I live blind within storm's eye, don't brood
on graveyard earth? I choose to self-delude.

Driftwood Fence

A life of float
laid on the sand
by onshore night wind

gifts of rake handles
with hammer ends
the boy gathers

embeds one end of each,
indeparallel pickets
of float that stand
against the tide.

Beach Comb

My hair is like the grass,
Both bending in the blow.

I bend for random gifts
That moving forces left:

Abandoned shells, and glass
That's sanded smooth, palm fronds,
Attractive wood, and junk-
All frizz on shoreline's head.

I palm my bleaching strands
And puzzle as I walk.

I try to compass all
There is in currents, winds,

And tides that flow through life.
Just then I'm stopped in stride

Before a circle laid
Upon the sand, a lei,

Hand-formed of tide-worn rocks,
Large beads in black and white,

A lava-coral beach
Array. I smooth the sand

And smooth my hair and choose
To lie inside this ring,

My head into the calm,
A compass of my own,

And point myself the way
To comb the mysteries out.

Towel Your Chair

Ranks of folding lounge chairs
All spaced in groups with gaps

Backs raised to the top notch
Backed against the pool fence,

Inside and out, with toes
Always toward the water,

Those on the lawn aligned
With vertically raked beach,

A beach unmarred by footsteps.
And a pool deck with no wet prints,

A scene set before sun time.
Each chair owned by a towel.

Finding Skill

Parking lot pennies and shells on the beach,
Gaining the image and where you should seek.

Whales in the ocean and planes in the skies,
Wanting to find it and moving the eyes.

Deer in the forest and shelves full of shoes,
A lifetime of practice with no mouse to use.

Crystal Parachutes

The
rain
drops
random-
ly arrived,
some finding
the lake and the
ground. Others were
delayed on people, roofs,
trees, streets or moving ob-
jects. And then there were the
special ones catching on the tele-
phone line. The angle of slope was
just right to make a rain swoop water
slide. Instead of rivering eaves and gut-
ters or soaking into soil, these drops did a
diamond dance, twinkling in a glory glide,
faceting light wobbling bright, slow paced
evenly spaced, gaining size in their ride
until their weight failed them and
they re-dropped reborn as
crystal parachutes.

Memory Flood

Sky throws down a coat of rain
splatting, supersaturating
and sliding off on a gravity roll
creasing steeply riverward
increasing in power
to roil soil, uproot trees, sweep yards
and ferry flotsam in a heightening
widening, accelerating flood, rushing
down.
Stream
beds in the valley bottom
receive a spreading, slowing flow
that browns green fields, reefs groves
enisles rises and roofs
while scattering floaters and settlers.
When the soaking storm subsides
the sun burns clear holes
through cloud vestiges, cheering a
child.
Hood
in hand, and restless
from endless penning, watching
the unebbing tide advance
the child throws on a raincoat
tugs on boots and runs to water's edge.
Obscured feet wade from the high water rock
to gather tidal detritus; light bulbs,
wooden boxes, plastic toys, decoys and driftwood
gathered on fence lines is a raft ride
away, a poled voyage over lapping rills
to harvest other treasures;
cedar logs, barn boards, a vagrant boat.

(no stanza break)

The child's pleasure in discovery
drowns deeper thoughts of flood destruction
as he reflects on the placid surface amid
the downstream childhood driftwood.

Boom Road

Have you been down the Boom Road lately?
Ancient graveled dust streak billowing
like a racing fuse, detonating
the sound storeroom at memory farm.
A whistling, rumbling, reminding boom.
Eerie otic pipe tones bring tingle
from a far warning of approaching
steam train slanting across fields. Steel wheel-whine.
A reverberating danger roar
heard through the feet. Don't play on the tracks!
Measured rail-end clacks. Double hollow
rattle over trestles. Mix of sounds
down trainlength peaking and receding.
There's a focusing wait for a blast
from the log dump announcing thunder.
Giant drum sticks beat timber "Taps",
tumbling from rail car down the decking.
Sudden surf of oceanic splash
rises from wood displacing water.
Boom boat pushes with a pocketa
engine. Caulk boots tunk firmly. Chains clank.
Pike poles chink into bark. Sledges chime
dogs into logs. Voices shout the song
of cooperative work, resting
only after rafting. Train chugs off
with lighter clicks. Dusty tires scratch
gravel as workers motor homeward.
Attic noises echo up the years
across the fields down the Boom Road.

No No's Tows

The noes
Were from woes
Chosen
From old tales
Of a relative
Who stuck an arm
Out a car window
And had it torn off
Or an acquaintance
Who was kicked in the head
Behind a work horse
And never was the same

Or a radio story
Of a girl who fell down
An old well
And died there
Or a man who peeked
Between two logs
When the dynamite
Went off
And lost an eye

Always one known example
To show that it was
Possible
Judy was running and tripped
And stuck the scissors in her eye
Grover sat on the back of the truck
And had both legs pinched off
Below the knees

That's how she hooked into her children
And towed them back inside the lines
Kept them out of harms way
Into straight
And narrow
Safe lives

Continuity

When I was very young
and spent the night at Grandma's house
I learned my home remained when I returned.

A week at 4-H camp
did not erase my bed or clothes
or change twice daily milking of the cows.

I knew the sun that rose
each day when I was at Fort Ord
would light the fields and buildings back at home.

Although I wasn't there
to watch, my family carried on
while I was off at school or traveling far.

The day my Grandpa died
I knew I still must go to work
each day providing for my family's needs.

When sun rose on his grave
my home remained to catch its rays
and family stirred to life in its warm light.

Barking Lesson

My grandmother was told by her father
that if she stopped to kick
at every little dog that ran out to bark at her
she'd never get anywhere in life.

She passed the story on to me,
and I learned to ignore the barking
except from the little dog
I found inside.

The Sentinel's Favorite

The dog and I are on a mound
Upon the grass beside the path.
I sit enjoying people pass.
He's on his stomach looking bored.

But then he stands in full alert,
A sudden pose with dog show freeze.
His tail's straight up, his chest pushed wide,
His ears a pair of arrowheads.

I am behind and cannot see
His eyes, but sighting with his tail
And nose I look beyond to find
Two poodles and, or course, they're white.

Andy's Shoes

Always fit and measured
By certified shoe men,
Right foot half size larger,
The width a double E.
Each new pair a triumph
Against depression pain.

Memories of childhood
And cardboard soles in holes.
Each year only one pair,
Even though his feet grew.
Toes that were misshapen
With inward turning nails.

Those flapping walks to school,
Discolored socks all wet.
Cold that rose like tree sap
And chills from being teased.
Rich kids all had good shoes
He saw with downcast eyes.

Money went for taxes,
Insurance, heat and food,
Gas that got Dad to work.
And shoes were just a frill.
He'd have barefoot summers
When shoes just didn't last.

Then right before school time
The shoe year came again.
And with sacrifices
From the family budget
There would be a new pair,
Maybe this year oxfords.

Each year they'd last longer
Because of careful steps
Growing up by walking
Till he graduated.
Then he earned his own way
And started buying shoes.

Sturdy leather work shoes
Laced above the ankles,
Polished every evening,
Ready for the next day,
Sitting in his closet
With fifty other pairs.

Each one worn with great pride.
Each a sign of richness.
For wealth has many meanings
And Andy lives with one
Always having new shoes
To walk away the past.

For Keeps

We played the game for keeps,
cats-eyes and crockies
shooter-struck from eye-shaped pots
drawn by chalk on blacktop
or scratched by sticks in dirt
where grit ground into knuckles
and knees ground through jeans.

My first bag of twenty went fast,
and there was no money
for something I'd just lose, so
I bore my loss for a year
until blackberry picking time
when I squirreled away coins
to make my next purchase
at the Little Store near school.

Meantime I studied what
the big boys did to win, practiced
their grip, steadied my hand,
learned speeds and spin, how to lag,
when to take rounders, schemed
about skill levels, who not
to play, who I might beat,

so when I played again
I won and kept a thousand,
and didn't need to buy
more marbles.

Ice Hockey

The ice on the lowland pond
Sags in the center
But it's thick and doesn't creak
Or crack under our leather soles

As we dare each other farther out.
This is a first for us young boys
The only time we've known five days
Below twenty degrees. We've used up

And broken apart all of the ice
In mud puddles near our houses
So this is the next step, new ice
Big ice, ice hockey ice.

It holds as we walk across.
It supports running and sliding.
So we gather sticks from the woods nearby
Breaking limbs that have bends

Resembling hockey sticks
That we've only seen in pictures.
And who can think of what
We'll use for a puck?

A rock might do, but better
Would be an Eveready flashlight battery
With a pasteboard cover. And so we played
One long glorious game until we got too cold

And fell too many times and made too many cracks
And beat the battery apart
And in our innocence made a memory
That held like the ice on that singular day.

Where We Danced

When rock and roll was still learning its name
a darkened room with saxophone band or
jukebox was all it took to have a dance.

In days when Crewcuts, Comets and Crickets
were on forty-fives, somewhere you could find
a dance on Friday and Saturday nights.

The little gym had a slippery floor
from sprinkled soap flakes, and the last dance was
Al Hibler singing "Unchained Melody".

The Eagles (Ruby's place), boys on one side,
girls the other, nervous to cross the floor.
Skokian, Sh-Boom and Goodnight Sweetheart.

The Harb with its turning glitter ball,
skating to records one night, dancing the next,
sometimes a live band like the Beachcombers.

Harms out at Westport wreathed in briny air.
Musty sake hay smell of Tuntland's barn.
A Swisser at Menlo, schottische, polka.

Any high school after a game sock hop.
Claquato, The Tropics, the Oakville Grange,
Evergreen Ballroom, The Spanish Castle.

Fleetwoods at the Olympia Odd Fellows,
Kingsmen, The Wailers, Little Bill's Bluenotes.
Bop, jitterbug, dirty boogie, gator.

I saw you dancing in the gym.
Working on mysteries without any clues.
You don't know what you been missing, oh boy.

Synchronizing a whole generation.
Picking our partners for life
by the way we fit and felt when we danced.

A Long Line

It's a family vacation, three sons and a dad
doing some fishing and hunting in Alaska. First day
the four take the boat out late for shrimp. They start
to drop the pots on a long line. Something common
happens. The line gets in the prop. Experience
says there are twenty seconds to grab the axe
and chop the line. There's really no choice.

But you're the son who built this boat, who paid
for the line and the pots, who knows these waters,
and you're the one who always beats danger.
So you reach to untangle the prop and you don't see
how fast the stern is pulled down by the sinking pots,
so when the icy water starts pouring into the boat
it's already too late.

Of course you have no survival suit on. As the boat fills
and starts to sink you look at your two brothers and your dad
and shrug, and step off with your boots on. And as you sink
you take those three gulps of water and never know
that you'll drown alone in Hoona Sound.

One brother with a life jacket dies numb and is found
washed up miles away. Your dad grabs a fish box cover
and holds on, while your other brother somehow
propels the two of them (through that water that kills
in ten minutes) for half an hour and half a mile
to a shallow point where both drag out to the treed beach.

And both survived. To live every day with that cold water on them, hearing one cry of help across the water, and knowing to live on they have to forget somewhat, yet if they do they fail their family again. So they will always have thoughts of Alaska. And will they go back where shrimp might fish for them?

And here I am sitting on the life raft box of an Alaska ferry passing through Hoona Sound on a clear day with flat water, wondering.

Night Voices

A mile down the hill along the river
voices of the hog and the wood chipper
converse in the night across dead air.
The hog speaks of bark and sap, connoisseur
of oil of cedar, pitchy gummy fir,
bitter hemlock juice and staining alder.
It snarls of bark for gardens as it rips
logs smooth to ready them for foreign ships.
The gnashing chipper with twenty-two teeth
slashing inside its circular mouth
says varied densities and textures count
when chewing fibrous wood in great amounts.
It yelps at knots and hidden wire and nails,
while filling barges, stacking chips in piles.
The night enlivens with the noise of work,
the voices of machines that grind and clank,
growl and whir in their metallic tones
that echo from the bluff through tidal zones
and carry up landfolds to where I lie,
eavesdropping beneath my cedar roof.

Woven Baskets

In these woven baskets is the gather of a lifetime
Handiwork of skilled hands that worked in nature's store

Gathered from the forest by the milky Quilcene River
Gathered from the salt marsh of Puyallup's tidal shore

Working with the cattails that are woven like a whole cloth
Working into spruce root, dyed designs just like on paper

Weaving in the camas lore, weaving in spirit figures
Weaving in the raven's cry, weaving in salmon wisdom

Holder of the woven robe, berries dried and meat smoked
Holder of the hunt and gather, wisps of smoke from cedar longhouse

This one holds the message of the language of the land
This one bears the hands that wove the basket woven in

Hometown

Where I live its always clean.
Flowers bloom and grass is green.

Paint is fresh and streets are swept.
All around my town's well kept.

Here there's sun and never rain
Falling on my peaceful lane.

People pass with friendly smiles
Walking through the winding aisles.

Pleasant are the sounds I hear,
Constant hum of buzzing cheer.

People nod and wait their turns.
This is what a good life earns.

There's so much to see and do
Every day it seems brand new.

It's a place where spirits soar.
When I leave I miss it more.

This is where I'm never down.
Disneyland is my hometown.

Label Day

Onya greets me from behind Ray-Bans.
I have on my Cadillac cap, Microsoft shirt.
We have met at Charles' on Broadway
for Glenlivet and Talking Rain.

As we enter I notice the Nordstrom label
outside the sweater wrapped around her neck.
I've never learned to read internal tags.
She stores her first impression of me knowing

that clothes make the man.
An empty garbage can
beside the bar accepts my Starbucks cup.
Onya sits near the Redhook sign.

She asks about my sign.
I speak of Coca Cola, Boeing.
We chat with little I contact
yet see the companies we keep.

Carwash Bird

The advertiser
In the Wal-Mart lot
Floats her siren song
Through the car park line
  Car wash   Car wash
Stands on the curb
In a club t-shirt
Wet from the wash work
With a felt-penned sign, calling
  Car wash   Car wash
Get your free carwash
Donations accepted
A sponge wash by hand
And for a good cause
  Car wash   Car wash
With hoses and soap suds
As her blacktop backdrop
The carwash bird preens
And chirps her come-on call

Latte Motion

Walking with a triple twenty
clutched before me like a flag staff
my palms spread desert warmth
while my toes warn of cold.

Bending to the cylinder
I recall an oval window in an oak door
and a wooden wishing well
before dropping an old penny.
The coin's taste competes
with burning leaves and honey
as I swallow.

City and weather recede
as memories and warmth flood within.
My feet wade through long ago mud puddles.
Toast is in my mouth. A Sunday roast fills me.
My mood is a brown study.

Only the changing light urges me on.

Box Score

Today I toted twelve
  And others carried more.
    Our score was fifty-four.

We filled the boxes
  In advance, commodities
    That came to forty pounds.

This Friday was the third,
  The monthly food bank day
    For seniors who need aid

And most are ladies who
  Consider this a treat,
    Dress and do their hair.

Some carpool from the Manor
  To sit and socialize
    Well before the scheduled time.

And we are there to carry out,
  For lack of strength,
    Fill in for those departed,

Spouse or distant child
  Give backto those who bore
    The burdens of the past

Depression, war, and family
  And carried us to now
    Blessed with enough and more

So we can try to even up
The score. And still their thank-yous
Seem to keep them ahead.

A Medi-Prescription

Dad handed me his bill from Medicare.
At ninety-three he fell, and hit his head,
then bled all night into the hallway rug.

He wasn't strong enough to stand, or pull
himself up to a telephone. "I am
a mess," he told my wife who went to check

on him next day. She called for help at nine
one one, and soon the ambulance arrived.
His stay for care was just three days. The bill

was fourteen thousand bucks. Dad said
to me, "I am not worth that much." And I
replied, "What would another option be?

Should we have left you bleeding on the rug,
or used the twenty-two you kept to kill
the ailing animals out on our farm?"

And in my failing years is that what I
look forward to, analysis of cost
and worth both factored in, and –care denied?

A Closing Door

Every day is a closing door
Sealing off the deepening past
Tighter than each day before
Cinching down to the very last.

Sealing off the deepening past
The fogs of memory thicken
Cinching down to the very last
At a pace that will only quicken.

The fogs of memory thicken
Entering behind a dark brow
At a pace that will only quicken
Interring the mind in the now.

Entering behind a dark brow
The thought thieves tighten the lock
Interring the mind in the now
Like hands on a frozen clock.

The thought thieves tighten the lock
Tighter than each day before
Like hands on a frozen clock
Every day is a closing door.

Drawer People

Existing in a folder filed in a closed drawer
out of sight, off the rolls, no count, no address, no face
no longer found in unemployment statistics
are the drawer people
relegated to the back of a bureaucrat's cabinet
because they are long unemployed, intractable cases
due to their lack of education, negligible job skills
and bouts of drug addiction.
                                        The back of the drawer
they live in is a back alley, back in the woods,
back window used to enter an empty house.
Job skills are alley scrounging, dumpster diving,
can collecting, panhandling in select locations.
Survival is their education; knowing food banks,
soup kitchens, shelters, clinics, the catalog of handouts.
Theirs is an active file on street survival.

Inside Outside

The rule lady
goes outside to fill a bucket
with water from the tap
because above the sink
inside the rest stop coffee shack
the rule sheet says,
"Water for coffee will be obtained from outside taps
and not from utility room faucets."

Common sense says
perked coffee is boiled water
and the water from the inside sink faucet
should be okay.
So the words of the rule roil inside me
demanding explanation.

I call the WSDOT permit person
who says
in their terminology
the only inside water
is the water inside the bathroom.
Everything else is outside.

So the water from the faucet
at the sink inside
the coffee shack is outside
and it's safe
to put inside your body, though
the water inside the bathroom
is not to be drunk.

So I wash the face value of words
with outside water
to get inside their meaning.
The rule lady
is awash with indignation,
while I am inside-watered off with WSDOT, period.

Man Fun

Go get the sawsall.
Hack up the hot tub.
Chunk it in sections.
Fill up the dumpster.

Cord start the chain saw.
Cut up the blow down.
Section the log rounds.
Split up the firewood.

Hook up the water.
Power wash the roof moss,
The slime off the wood steps,
The black from the concrete.

Go rent a jack hammer.
Crack through the concrete.
Pound out some loud noise.
Vibrate your muscles.

Bring home a backhoe.
Chew down the building.
Bite off big wood chunks.
Push down the chimney.

Get that machinery.
Make lots of proud noises.
Let's have some man fun
Playing destruction.

Sweat Jobs

Muscle work, walk and lift
Labor at reach and pull
Push and carry in heat
Humid with high hot sun

Pickle smelling hatband
Face lined by dust deltas
Legs held in shrinkwrap pants
Nose is a sweat faucet

Wheelbarrow of concrete
Sheetrock up a ladder
Pulling off the green chain
Fir trees planted up hill

Not enough water breaks
Thirty minutes for lunch
Sandwiches taste funny
In a honey bucket

Not lulled to siesta
Machines that whirl and grab
Are sharp and threatening
Strong deodorant fails

Six pack on the way home
Clothes shed inside the door
Hot bath cleanses the ache
Recliner and remote

Bryan's Song

The chains Bryan ground hang on the nail
waiting for me, the saw, and the wrench.
I know if I use them I honor his skill,
but when they are dull he is gone.

So the Bryan-ground chains remain on the nail.
But one day soon when I know it's right
I'll pull down those chains and grab the saw
And we'll go cut some f---ing trees.

Blacktop Strip

The news report on the radio says
a van that carried a cross-country team
hit a free-range horse
on the Warm Springs Reservation.

The black top strip
holds the movement of men
in a black plague one-ton life erasers
going seventy, and keeping no body count.

There are fences to keep the snow off,
fences to protect the meat cows,
and a fence around the lot of dead iron pickups
but none to slow wild animals.

The deer warning sign
has the usual bullet holes.
The strip crosses the deer land.
And the deer aren't warned.

Three crows fly from a flat raccoon,
living on death, picking
the strip clean, leaving a chip
seal of bone chips.

Three slim white
crosses stand in a berm.
Still hawks wait
above the roadside zone.

It's a culture of animal sacrifice
with black tires on black
tar, colored with blood-rust.
Just one last kiss for the blacktop God

with a tributes of feathers,
fur, and skunk odor.
That's human progress from sea
to sea and border to border.

Reception and Engagement

A neighbor's getting hitched at the First Methodist.
Have to get out the tractor with the sickle mower
to ready the field. Need lots of room for parking,
folding tables from back stage of the Grange,
chairs from the I. O. O. F. Wheel in the split oil-drum
barbecue, roast a pig and let it sizzle and drip.
Homemade rolls. Potato salad sitting in the sun.
Beer keg in a washtub of ice with lots of volunteers
to testing the brew and man the pump. Fancy woven wood
picnic baskets with fried barnyard chickens and baked beans.
Line up to kiss the bride or groom, get a slice of cake.
Sit around and jaw, pass the news. Start up a softball game.
Couple up and slip away to the trees down by the creek.

The Dead Man Memorial at Seaside, Oregon

At Seaside south and minus one point five
after reading the Dead Man Memorial
I walk down
to where boulder beach
and sandy shore ell
to a head-shaped ebb
where extreme debris has pooled;
whelks and wormwood, luminous bones
that I view through a limpet keyhole,
broken glass, crab backs,
and tidal tea-leaf beach grass pushed up the slope,
and left behind,
where I scallop the water's edge,
keeping my side to the tide and my shoes
dry, continuing my everstudy
of lapping spill, tuning
to the lace of waves
and lore of salt and tide pulsing in my ears,
learning when the waves aren't right
so I won't be Found
on the Beach
by seeking sneaker waves.

Watching the War

I watch
The damaged tank
Fume in the road
As soldiers
Move hurt
At the turret
Dazed
But slowly
Stirring

One stands
Calls
To others
Attends
To a man
Draped
From a hatch
Struggles
To rouse help
To move
The still soldier
To the ground

It seems
I watch
Forever

I want
To help
But I
Am on the other side
Of the world

I wonder why
There is no one

Around this blown up tank
Either
To attack
The injured crew
Or offer help

At last
Crew members move
The still soldier
To the ground
And give frantic aid

And in the end
He lies
In a circle
Of bowed heads

I saw it all
Through a steady eye
And though I shouted
Across the world
For the video man
To drop his tool
And offer human aid
The picture never
Stopped
Nor even trembled

Fishing In Confusion

She reels me in and casts me back.
Her hook is snelled and quells my speech.
The thought of slough stays on my tongue.
Upon her voice I'm pierced and dazed.
I taste her tone. It floods my eyes.
She takes me down beside the tide.
She angles with a velvet lure.
A lurid idea comes with her hook.
An ouzel bobs approval. It
may change my mind. She casts a stone
upon the flow. Ironwood it is,
but on the surface it does skip.
Hers is a heart-shaped stone of love.
My heart does skips. I walk on water.
Precious she is. She deeply sinks
in reflection, to rise allured
by weighty promise: a promise that's
a barbed hook for castaways
joined on an ever winding reel.

With Gravity

Morning sun crests the roof
Adding light to the newspaper.
I sit in the lawn chair
Beneath the tall cottonwood
And read of discoveries about gravity,
That the speed of light
Equals the speed of gravity,
And as I read and ponder
The earth turns the sun
Up into the leaves of the tree
And the slow twist of shade
Gradually consumes me.
Gravity at 185,000 miles per second
Pulls all over me.
Light at 185,000 miles per second
Bombards part of me.
And I can't feel a thing
Or tell a difference.
Maybe it's the force of shade on my head
That keeps me from understanding
The situation of the gravity.

Fall Lights

Hitting the turf
the oblong football
bounced oddly

amid a bi-colored churn,
and the scoreboard icon
shifted possession across.

The football-phase moon
rolled above the scoreboard
in a slow punt,

lighting the field
and the moving uniforms,
icons all of the rising fall.

Solstice

At sunset
Of summer's
First day
                A hint
Of winter
Slaps at me
From the lake
                        Where
A skier's
Last fast ride
On taut line
                     Turns
From out wide
As the arc
Starts back.

River Tea

fall leaves
teeter down
to clear river

float like boats
curl in swirl
and mix under

leach
and leak
a toning tincture

teaing
downstream flow
to tannin tones

The Salmon Fishery

The fisher releases the brake with his hand,
And the net reels out from the bowpicker's wheel
Fifty fathom across on the channel tide,
With floats at the surface, weights twenty feet down.

The net reels out from the bowpicker's wheel
As the salmon swim in their natural way
Between floats at the surface, weights twenty feet down
While the gulls circle and call in the sky.

The salmon swim in their natural way,
And the drift net rides the upstream tide
While the gulls circle and call in the sky
O'er the roundhead shine of a seeking seal.

The drift net rides the upstream tide
As the salmon push their heads through the net
Ahead of the shine of a seeking seal,
And the swift-swimming fish are trapped at their gills.

As the salmon push their heads through the net
There's a pulling down of fluorescent floats.
The strong-swimming fish are trapped at the gills
And the fisherman stands and smiles in his boat.

There's a pulling down of fluorescent floats
As the seal dives in his natural way,
And the fisherman stands and frowns in his boat
As a float bobs higher in the flowing stream.

As the seal dines in his natural way
The boat rides the flow with the cross-channel net.
As a float bobs higher in the flowing stream
The fisherman yearns for the end of the drift.

The boat rides the flow with the cross-channel net,
And the gill-caught salmon thrash their tails
As the fisherman reaches the end of the drift
And reels in the catch with the winding winch.

The gill-caught salmon thrash their tails
As the fisherman acts in his natural way
Reeling in the catch with the winding winch,
Pulling fish by hand from the dripping net.

The fisherman acts in his natural way
As the net is wound on the turning spool,
Pulling fish by hand from the dripping net
While a float bobs high in a tinge of red.

As the net is wound on the turning spool
There's one less fish in the shortening length,
While a float bobs high in a tinge of red
And the gulls drop down to feed at the net.

And there's one less fish in the shortening length
As the fisherman works the winch with his foot,
And the gulls drop down to feed at the net
Twenty fathom across on the channel tide.

Seascape with Glass Ball

Fragile on rocky coast, it is strong in soft sea
Holding in place the fate of fish and fisherman
Until washed from boat deck or torn by storm
From binding net to Kuroshio where it will ride

An endless carousel of sea and time, circling
The north Pacific till brisk west wind and high tide
Release it to the ease of sandy shore, finally free
Like the artist there to record its arrival.

On Cedar Beach

It stimulates the appetite
To cook outside surrounded by
A rug of green with trees for walls
And roof of sky with air that's new

And bears the scent of flame-cooked food
On paper plates that rest upon
A tabletop that's made of glass
Through which I see my cedar beach.

Real Estate

Just listed
A great opportunity
For immediate occupancy
City view

Freeway front
Southern exposure
Through a cracked window
Eighty square feet

Underlayment floor
And a half bath
Utilities include
A hanging bulb

Two plug-ins
And a heat vent
Door needs repair
Walk on in for a look

A Hoodie for the Hoodoos

There are times when words come back to me,
Like my granddad saying growing old takes courage.
This day I see that time of courage can come
At any age for those who love.

A grieving family gathered at the church.
They were celebrating a well-lived life.
The oldest son, in middle age, spoke long
With feeling for the father who had passed.

One grandchild who sat in front, looked around,
Rose, and hurried back to sit by his dad.
He leaned close and pulled up his hoodie
While death paid him a special call.

The Name of the Beast

There's a beast within that I can't deny.
Its roar from my depths is always the same.
It whispers to me, "If you tell, you'll die."

I answer it with an animal cry.
Its call to me sets my mind aflame.
There's a beast within that I can't deny.

With body and soul is how I reply.
How do I battle a beast I can't name?
It whispers to me, "If you tell, you'll die."

I constantly think about schemes to try.
I bargain with it to make it be tame.
There's a beast within that I can't deny.

Each promise I make I know is a lie.
My struggle inside is ever my shame.
It whispers to me, "If you tell, you'll die."

I know when it calls that I must comply.
How do I conquer a thing with no name?
There's a beast within that I can't deny.
It whispers to me, "If you tell, you'll die."

Meltdown

In deep, dark vaults is kept the silent count
of past outrages crammed within the file
of disappointments that create a pile
that daily nears some critical amount.
Presents never sent. A false conclusion.
Promises made, not kept. Sweet words delayed.
Neglects and overlookings. All arrayed
as Did and Didn't, building heat of fusion.
The past provides a pale or brighter share
to present situations, that are fed
on current deeds or words that power care
by which today's relationship is read.
In crunch times, when neglectfulness does strike,
without Love's core it might be hard to Like.

A Late Surprise

I'm surprised I get to do this,
Go to the ocean in mid-October
When the thermometer says sixty-seven.
I sit on the balcony to watch sunset.

I am surprised I get this treat.
I never imagined it in my youth.
I didn't have time when I worked.
It just happened when I got older.

I am surprised that the wind quiets
So the gulls fly easy up the beach,
And the one on my railing
Will accept a Ritz from my fingers.

Then pelicans hover and dive.
Whale spouts hang in the offshore air
And the half sun is pale yellow
Across the sea shimmer of my surprise.

A Biker Retires

It’s a slope
That slants away before you
As you ride
And in the lasting glide
You’re as the wind
That pillows on your face
And the sun that hugs your back
And you stay in the flow
Coasting on and on

But sometime as you go
Unnoticed
                    The slope tips
So the coast becomes a climb
And the heat of effort
Builds into your mind
Until you know it’s time
And then
You gear down

Follow-Up

Quite early in that first grade year
a teacher said about one boy
that you could write his name in ink
above a city jail cell door.

Now we all hoped it wasn't true,
and tried each day to give to him,
and all the other kids, the kinds of skills
they'd need to keep them from that fate.

This happened forty years ago.
And still each week I read the list
the paper prints of people booked
into that city jail, and when

I see my students there, I find
I'm not surprised by who they are,
and tell myself that those not named
are living lives of great success.

Living Will

You knew the contents of my purse,
so I figured when you let yourself in
with the key above the meter box
you'd find this. I always wanted
to run my own affairs which was
a frustration to you. So here are all
the things I wouldn't tell you.
Bankbooks are under the carpet
under the bed. The checkbook
is in the plastic bin marked flour.
Deeds, insurance policies, and the number
of my lawyer who's expecting your call
are in the safety deposit box. Its key
is taped to the base of the living room lamp.
The recipe folder at the front
of the second file drawer has the red
book that lists what I own. Your favorite
ring is with other jewelry in the fourth
shoe box from the bottom at the back
of my closet. It's all your worry now.
I hope you'll forgive my stubbornness, with love.

Swallowing Pride

Tonight I was waterboy
For the poetry reading,
Fetching the stacked plastic cups
And ice water filled pitchers

And though I only listened
I drank in the successes
Of the readers and their poems
For all their voices were clear.

White Boat

Out of the dark
It stands
Lined in a tide
And still

Focused
In the frame of night
And living
Till the ebb of my look

When I recede
On a sudden flood
From the awareness
Of singularity.

Kathy Was

Kathy loved to go new places,
loved the strangeness, loved the going,
felt adventure in the moving,
got such pleasure from exploring.

Now she's on a new different journey
walking circuits in a hall
rubbing name plates by the door sides
re-exploring just a small space.

Where she is she can't remember.
Where she is we cannot join her.
What she was she isn't now.
We can't share her new adventure.

Eleven P. M. Forecast

My eyes shine
 from the five golden orbs
Seeing golden moments
 forelit in days to go

With time aplenty
 for cure and bale of hay
Then an evening's
 wash of chaff in a golden pond

And a picnic for sure
 on a day of rest
When golden grain
 is off the field

When ripe fruit
 is gone from golden boughs
And put away
 for the golden years

Where I can bask
 in the gleam of a sunny smile
In a silence
 that, of course, is golden.

Lantern Dig

At the horizon
are starry sky
and lantern string
hinged
like the bivalves
diggers seek
at ocean's edge.

Cactus Sunset

Red clouds band
in the sun city west
as I watch
the gold glow sink

look through verticals
that stand in softness
and fade
into the day dim

then reappear
in a last flash
of ambulance
and coyote yowls.

Art Escapio, or the Mystery of Poetry

When young I was curious to know the neighbor
who lived down the road. He seemed to work odd hours.
Cold mornings I'd find his footprints in rime, already
come or gone before I walked to school. The sharp line
of his profile sometimes found a momentary window
as I passed. But mostly I formed his image playing
with his children. Their welcoming smiles were as his face
to me. Their attire had quality, more lasting than stylish,
that became his person. His voice was in their speech,
words that ran from playful fun to careful truth.
With few worry lines they still showed respect for rules,
going in in the right time. Although I only sketched him
from his progeny I was sure he'd fit his image
if I found him coming toward me, someone I met before.

www.ingramcontent.com/pod-product-compliance
Lightning Source LLC
LaVergne TN
LVHW021541080426
835509LV00019B/2764